MODERN SPEED RECORD SUPERSTARS

MODERN
SPEED RECORD
SUPERSTARS

Ross R. Olney

Illustrated with photographs

DODD, MEAD & COMPANY
NEW YORK

PICTURE CREDITS

Photographs in this book are used through the courtesy of Dan Bisher, Rocketman Productions, Inc., 94, 99, 102-103, 104, 106, 108; Doug Freeman, 11; Freeman/McCue Public Relations, 78, 84, 86, 88, 90-91; Goodyear Tire and Rubber Company, 8, 64, 68, 72, 75, 76; Lockheed-California Company, 50, 53, 60; Ross R. Olney, 33; Doug Rose, 12-13, 34, 39, 41, 45, 46; Wayne Thoms, 10, 19, 20, 23 (by Lester Nehamkin), 26, 28-29, 30-31; U.S. Air Force, 48, 54, 56-57.

Copyright © 1982 by Ross R. Olney
All rights reserved
No part of this book may be reproduced in any form
without permission in writing from the publisher
Printed in the United States of America

1 2 3 4 5 6 7 8 9 10

Library of Congress Cataloging in Publication Data

Olney, Ross Robert, 1929-
   Modern speed record superstars.

   Includes index.
   Summary: Profiles six people who have set speed
records on land, on water, and in the air.
   1. Speed record holders—Biography—Juvenile litera-
ture. [1. Speed record holders] I. Title.
GV1019.046   796.7 [B] [920]   82-7400
ISBN 0-396-08072-3   AACR2

The author would like to thank the following for advice and technical information for this book and for the exciting photographs:

Dan Bisher, Rocketman Productions; David Densmore, National Hot Rod Association; Capt. Robert G. Ellis, U.S. Air Force, Beale AFB; Doug Freeman, Freeman/McCue Public Relations; David Hederich, Goodyear Tire and Rubber Company News Bureau; Doug Rose, Propulsion Enterprises; Dave Severson, Freeman/ McCue Public Relations; Bill Spaniel, Lockheed-California Company; and especially Deke Houlgate of Riverside International Raceway for the right guidance at the right moment, and Wayne Thoms of *Datsun Discovery* magazine for working with me so generously on this book.

**With best wishes for splendid good
luck to those who have set records,
and those who will**

CONTENTS

Foreword   9

1   Bob Summers   16

2   Doug Rose   32

3   Lt. Col. Eldon Joersz   47

4   Craig Breedlove   63

5   Lee Taylor   79

6   Gary Gabelich   93

Index   109

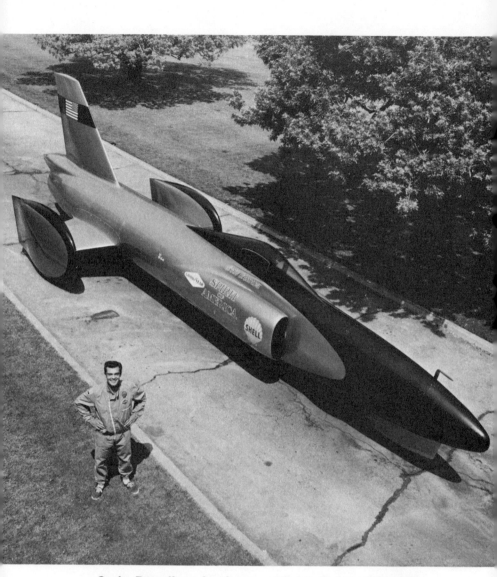

Craig Breedlove is shown with his Spirit of America, a land speed record car.

8

FOREWORD

There was a time not that long ago when people thought that going fast would kill you. Not because you might crash. That could happen, of course. No, they thought that the *speed alone* would kill you.

So the scientific ones made a careful study. Two miles per minute was the "killing" speed. That was the speed that was chemically dangerous. Nobody could go 120 miles per hour without deadly chemical changes in the body.

This was less than 100 years ago. Now humans have gone much faster without any chemical dangers. But speed has always been

The Summers brothers' Goldenrod still holds the land speed record for wheel-driven cars.

dangerous. It will always be dangerous.

Yet there are speed records for all types of vehicles. There is a speed record for bicycles, for skateboards, and even for roller skates. There are speed records for automobiles and airplanes and boats, and for spaceships.

It seems that every time somebody invents some new way to get around, somebody else sets a speed record with it. If it moves, a record can be set.

10

There are dozens and dozens of speed records for cars alone. There are dozens more for airplanes and boats. Records are kept for each type of car, for each engine, for each model and each design. People have always been interested and involved in speed.

Why do people try to set speed records?

Making money is always one reason. The fastest person of all can usually make some money from the record. The driver can take his car on tour and be paid a lot of money. People will pay just to look at the car that set a record. The pilot can take his airplane and the boat

Lee Taylor's U.S. Discovery II came to a tragic end.

driver his boat, and be paid. Speed record holders in the higher speeds are heroes wherever they go. They have dared death and survived. And much has been learned about vehicle performance as a result. This information can help everybody improve their own vehicles.

So money is not the only reason for speed records. It can't be, especially in the faster classes. Drivers design and build, and worry

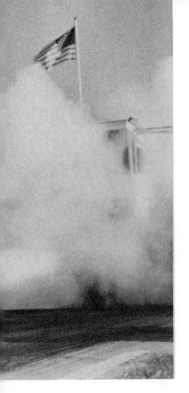

The fastest jet on a drag strip is Doug Rose's Green Mamba.

and fret, and take chance after chance to set a record. They come back again and again to try. They put their lives on the line again and again. They keep trying — through broken parts and serious accidents. They often lose friends and family because of their passion for speed.

Sometimes they use all of their money. And all of their assets. And all the money they can borrow from all of their friends and sponsors. They keep trying and trying and trying.

Nowhere else in sports are participants so dedicated as in the sport of world speed records.

Many lose their lives in the attempts.

They go for the record for the same reason that people climb mountains or swim great distances. Because it is there to be done. There seems to be no other really sound reason.

For water speed records they look for flat, smooth, windfree water with enough room to make a long speed-up and slow-down run. For air speed records they look for the smoother air generally found in the western United States.

For land speed records they generally go to the great salt flats called Bonneville Salt Flats in Utah. This immense wasteland of flat salt is large enough and smooth enough for the job. A long speed-up area can be smoothed and prepared. So can a long slow-down area. Between the two are the "traps," the exactly measured mile and kilometer where the record speed counts.

Part of the year the salt flats are covered by water. The rest of the year they are used by one team after another to go for one record or another.

In this book only the very fastest are considered. The fastest on land in wheel-driven cars (Bob Summers), in jet cars (Craig Breedlove), and in rocket cars (Gary Gabelich) are here. So is the fastest in jet cars on a drag strip (Doug Rose). So is the fastest on water (Lee Taylor) and the fastest in the air (Lt. Col. Eldon Joersz).

These men have gone faster than anybody else in the world in their own type of vehicle.

1

BOB SUMMERS

Try to imagine a speed of 400 miles per hour on land. Imagine you are in a piston-engine, wheel-driven vehicle.

The engine is roaring and the ground is rushing by. You are as much flying low as driving on the ground. This is, in fact, the oldest of all the land speed records. Almost as soon as the second automobile was built, the thought of racing came into the minds of the men who built them.

Then somebody thought of going for top speed — flat-out speed. How fast could a vehicle go if there were no limit to how large the engine was? Or no limit to how big the course was? The speeds began to climb.

They were breakneck speeds in the minds of the people setting them. They edged up from 35 to 50 miles per hour. Then 60 and 70. Today, most of us have gone that fast in a car. Yet at one time these were speed records.

The records climbed on above 100 miles per hour. The sand of Daytona Beach was a popular place for record attempts. It was long and straight and smooth and hard-packed.

The speed rose to 200 miles per hour and then 300. Daredevil drivers began to imagine 400 miles an hour in a wheel-driven vehicle.

These were not jet or rocket cars. They were not wingless airplanes. These were *real* cars, with transmissions and engines.

But 400 miles per hour became a great barrier for these cars. By 1965 only three men in the history of speed records had reached it.

The great English driver John Cobb came to lonely Bonneville Salt Flats in 1947. He managed to run faster than 400 mph on one of his two passes through the traps. His final average speed was 394.2 miles per hour. (Speed record cars must make the run one way, then make the run back, so that wind and other factors are averaged out. Two complete passes are necessary.)

American champion Mickey Thompson took his low-slung, four-engined Challenger up to 406.6 at Bonneville. But he was unable to complete a return run, so the record was not official. This was in 1959.

in 1964, Britain's Donald Campbell drove his Bluebird to an average speed of 403.1 on an Australian dry lake bed. Later he was killed trying to set a water speed record. But he held the land speed record for wheel-driven vehicles.

These were the only drivers in history to have roared this fast over land in a regular car — if you could call any of these sleek streamliners "regular."

Even as Sir Donald Campbell was setting his record in Australia, two brothers were dreaming of the record. They lived in Southern California, where so many of the speed stars

18

The Summers brothers, Bob (left) and Bill.

come from. They had no money, only a dream—
and one other thing. Each brother had a great
talent for car building. And for getting the most
speed out of a car.

They were Bill and Bob Summers. Bill was
the oldest at 29. He had a detail mind. He could
keep records and handle money. He could look
to all the problems of a land speed record
attempt. Bill became the team manager as well
as working as a mechanic and builder.

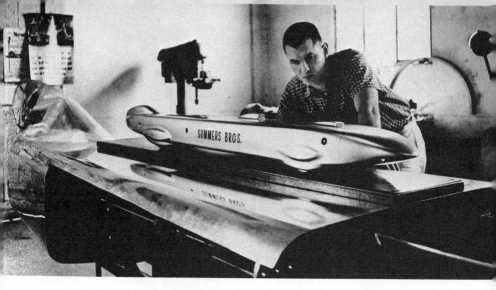

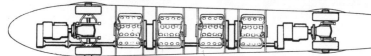

Bob Summers looks over the model of Goldenrod as it sits on the long, gleaming hood of the real car. Below is the diagram of the engine layout.

Bob, the younger brother, was 28. He was the engine expert. He *knew* engines. He had a feel for them. He figured he could hook up four powerful engines in one car and break the land speed record. Bob's nickname was "Butch." Butch would drive the car.

The brothers decided to name their speed record car Goldenrod. They built a model of the car. It was a beautiful model of a car that would be long and low and sleek. It would be 32 feet long with tight-fitting, smooth body panels. There would be four powerful Chrysler Hemi engines in a row in the car.

But it is a long way between building a model of a land speed record car and building the car. The man who is going to risk his life to drive one of them still needs the financial help of others to build one.

Companies involved in automobiles are asked for money quite often. But how do they tell between a serious record attempt and somebody who just wants to play around? Getting money for a record attempt is almost impossible.

The Summers brothers knew this. But they knew they had to try. Bob started the round of possible sponsors.

"We're interested," sponsors would say. "If you can sign up other sponsors, we'll go along."

Such persons could see that the Summers brothers had a solid proposal. Bill and Bob Summers had done their homework well. They had a model of a car that could do the job. Sponsors could see that the brothers might even break the long-standing speed record for wheel-driven vehicles. They wanted their names to be connected with such an attempt if it appeared it might be successful.

But more than one sponsor was needed.

Finally George Hurst of Hurst Performance Products said he would donate to the project. He could see that the brothers were serious. Soon Chrysler, Firestone, and Mobil Oil joined in and the project moved forward.

For one thing, the Summers brothers were not strangers to Bonneville Salt Flats. They had been racing there since 1954. They had raced on the famous California dry lakes (Muroc and El Mirage) before that. They were experienced. Bill had always concentrated on building, and Bob on driving. But Bill had driven very fast and certainly Bob was a fine builder. They were a team. They worked together very well, especially when the pressure was on.

Once Bob endured a horrible crash at Bonneville. The car they built had flipped over and

With Bob at the wheel, Goldenrod is tested at Riverside International Raceway in California.

over and skidded nearly one mile. It was one of the worst crashes ever seen on the salt flats. But Bob was OK and the car wasn't too badly damaged.

The problem was, how were they going to tell their mother about the crash? Every newsman there had seen it and was reporting it. She'd know soon, back in Southern California — probably as soon as the evening news was televised. It had been a spectacular crash.

So Bill called their mother. After several minutes of small talk, he came to the point. He was just fine and so was Bob. They missed her and would be seeing her soon. Then, just before he hung up, almost as though he had just thought of it, he said, "Oh, yeah, Mom, I forgot. Bob had a little accident today but it was nothing serious. He wasn't scratched and the car's going to be OK."

"That's fine, son."

"Well, I gotta run now, Mom. Lots of work to do. Good-bye now."

At least when she heard the news she knew her boys were all right.

In October, 1963, Bob had set a national and international Class C record of 279.40 in the mile and in the kilometer. The brothers had built the record-setting car, Pollywog.

By 1965 the Goldenrod project was well under way. But money was always a problem. The brothers would build until they were broke, then go to their sponsors for more money. Gradually the long, sleek car took shape. They worked in shifts. Bob would come in at two in

the morning and work until five in the after-
noon. Bill would come in at eight in the morning
and work until late at night. Neither brother was
married, so they could spend most of their time
working on the car at these unusual hours.

On September 1, 1965, the car rolled out of its
trailer and onto the gleaming white salt at Bonneville. Within two hours the car had been
made ready and Bob squeezed into the cockpit.
He waved his hand, shouted "Let's go!" and
felt the bump as Bill eased their station wagon
up for a push. The car rolled forward.

But only three of the Goldenrod's engines
fired. So they adjusted linkages and tried again.
They drove through test after test. The course
was wet and sloppy. They needed 13 good clear
miles for a record speed run. But they had only
6. They had transmission problems. Then a uni-
versal joint failed.

Sponsors suggested they take their car back
to California and work out the bugs.

"No," said both brothers. They had reached a
speed of 244.9 on one test run. They knew they
were on the right track. Working in a hangar at

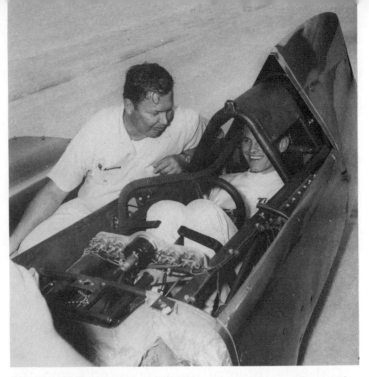

Bob and Bill were happy that the tests were getting under way at Bonneville Salt Flats.

nearby Wendover Air Force Base, they repaired Goldenrod.

Meanwhile, the weather was getting worse and worse. Once the rain starts at Bonneville, the speed runs are over for the year. Much of the course is underwater. So the brothers worked as hard as they could to solve their problems.

By mid-September they were more than

$15,000 in the hole. They knew that only a land speed record could help them. Once the car had set the record, it could go on tour. A land speed record car and driver can earn over $1,000 per day. But first the world land speed record must be set. And that is something very few people do.

On September 20, 12 miles of good salt became available. They rushed the car to the course. But a rainstorm came in and wiped out four miles. They waited.

On September 25 they were on the course. But Bob shut down the engines because he heard a strange noise. Then on the next run they had an electrical fire in the engine compartment. Then real disaster struck. Gears in the transmission failed. There were no spares. It appeared they were finished for the year.

Sadly, they packed up and headed for home. It was the next team's turn on the salt.

But Firestone man Jim Cook said, "You get home and get the car fixed. Get ready because you might be coming back this year."

Other drivers had the salt for awhile. But it

There were problems with Goldenrod, but the crew worked hard to correct them.

was possible that a few days might become available. The brothers worked 24 hours a day getting Goldenrod repaired.

Meanwhile, on the salt flats, Craig Breedlove set a land speed record for jet cars. Then Firestone had the salt again. Art Arfons broke Breedlove's record. Suddenly there were a few days available.

"You have the rest of the week," telephoned Jim Cook. "Come on up and try again."

The brothers arrived on the salt flats on Wednesday, November 10. Firestone had the salt for three more days. So they had three days left to set their record. Weather was threaten-

28

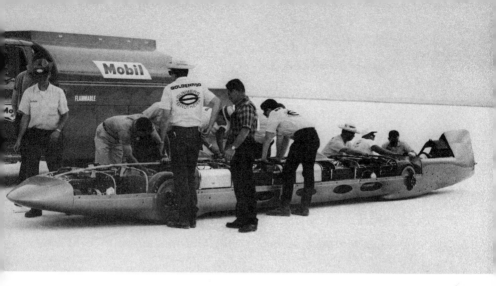

ing to close the flats for good. At noon on Thursday, the Goldenrod streaked through the measured mile.

The speed was flashed to the crew by radio. It was 400 miles per hour. But they couldn't make a return run because of an overheated wheel bearing. That night, they worked on the problem.

Friday morning was gray and gloomy. A light drizzle fell. The salt looked dull and angry. The Goldenrod was fired up. Soon it was thundering across the flats.

The first run was clocked at 412 miles per hour. Quickly the crew turned the car around

Goldenrod streaks through the measured mile at over

and refueled it for the necessary return run. Goldenrod roared away and flashed through the measured mile. The speed was 409.77. The Summers brothers were the new world land speed record holders for wheel-driven cars.

The crew pulled Bob from the cockput, hoisted him on their shoulders, and danced around. They had done it all in one year. It had never happened before in modern history so quickly.

There is a postscript to the Summers' story. Everybody knows about the speed record, for it still stands. It might stand forever, with land speed records so very expensive to achieve. Most speed record holders are now using jet

400 miles per hour.

and rocket cars. They are cheaper for the amount of power they produce.

There are rumors about new wheel-driven record attempts from time to time. But nobody has actually done it.

Bob Summers was convinced that the Goldenrod would go even faster. So the very next morning he made another run. His speed was over *425 miles per hour.*

But the record from the day before had already been flashed to the world. It was in all the newspapers. The Summers brothers decided to say nothing about this new record.

It hasn't mattered for many years, anyhow. No one has beaten either record.

2

DOUG ROSE

One of the most feared snakes in the world is the dreaded green mamba. The mamba is the fastest snake in the world. It can move through trees or on the ground at a lightning pace. The poison of the green mamba is so deadly that the African natives call it "90-second death."

Imagine this evil snake in the form of a dangerous vehicle.

Imagine a huge, heavy J-47 jet engine on wheels. This is the engine that was used in the Navy's F7U Cutlass fighter plane. It weighs several thousand pounds and is nearly 20 feet long.

Doug Rose

Now imagine a small, sleek cockpit attached in front of the giant air intake. The cockpit, with slitted, hooded eyes attached near the nose, is large enough to hold one man.

The entire body of the vehicle is painted with green scales. The vehicle has become a Green Mamba. There is another name painted on the cockpit, too. It is the name of the driver of this mean-looking machine. It is Doug Rose.

Jet car exhibition runs are among the most exciting events at a race track. But while other

The Green Mamba is a fearsome-looking car, and so is the driver's helmet.

dragsters seem to attract fans closer, jet cars frighten them away. When the driver of a jet car flips the switch, there is a roll of thunder and a flash of fire. Eveybody backs away to a safe distance. Nobody is ever sure whether the car will move forward or simply explode.

For several years Doug Rose drove Walt Arfons' Green Monster jet car. Arfons was a very famous land speed record driver. Most fans had heard of his Green Monster. Then Doug Rose designed and built his own Green Mamba. With the two cars, he has been the National Jet Car Champion for more than ten years.

But not without pain, and tragedy.

As a young boy, Rose dreamed of jet engines. Not in cars, but in flight. He was a fan of the astronauts and watched their feats on television. He would sit in his classroom at school in Milwaukee, Wisconsin, and dream of jet and space flight.

He went from school into the Navy. There he worked with jet planes. More and more he was drawn to the giant jet engines. He left the Navy

35

and became a truck driver for a paper company in Milwaukee. But as a hobby and because he had developed a skill with a camera, he became the track photographer at a local drag strip. Soon, other tracks took him on.

"My money wasn't really made selling pictures to the tracks," Rose said. "That was enough to pay for my gas and expenses. Then I would sell photos to the drivers and owners."

The roaring sport of racing and the young man who had dreamed about space and jet engines were coming closer and closer together. Rose liked the race tracks. He felt at home around racing people.

One day he met Walt Arfons. Arfons owned the Green Monster jet dragster. Rose took one look and knew what he wanted to do. He began to try to talk Arfons into letting him drive the big green car.

Meanwhile, he helped Arfons work on the car. The afterburner wasn't working just right. The car was on its way to California for some speed runs. Rose was able to help because of his jet experience in the Navy.

In 1962, Rose went to work for Walter Arfons as a helper and driver-trainee. Arfons had been looking for somebody and Doug Rose was the answer. Rose's only drag racing experience was with a 1953 flat-head engine. He had only amateur experience. He was perfect to learn the different techniques of driving a jet car on a drag strip. Arfons began to teach the young, inexperienced Rose.

Rose's first run before an audience was made in Florida a few months later. He was good and Arfons knew it. The crowds loved to watch Rose in the Monster. Still, Arfons was the number one driver. He would make the "real" runs. Then Rose would make a run or two for practice. The speeds then were about 130 miles per hour at the end of the quarter-mile strip.

More important was the great sound and fury and noise of the Green Monster. The crowds were often stunned. They demanded more and more. Finally, Rose made the first run at 200 miles per hour in a jet car on a drag strip.

"It was super," he recalled. "The [after]

burner lit and the car was running good. The acceleration is . . . is . . ." he paused. "Well, the car just keeps charging. It doesn't reach a point where it slacks off. It's pushing all the way until you shut it off." This was in the winter of 1962, in Arizona.

By 1963, Rose was driving the Green Monster full-time. He would go on the road by himself, leaving Arfons at home to manage the business. Rose would find a helper to run the pit for him at each track. Later, his wife served as his pit crew.

But everything didn't always go smoothly for the young driver and his jet car. Once, in Tampa, Florida, a parachute failed. Parachutes are needed to slow down jet cars after a run. Brakes would quickly burn out.

The Green Monster sailed through the air over a ditch and plowed nose first into the other side. It landed just short of a local highway, within the right-of-way. Guarding the ditch and the road had been a barbed-wire fence. One of the strands had cut Rose's goggles in two. Blood was streaming down his face from his

Parachutes are needed to slow down jet cars at the end of the drag strip.

eyes. He was frightened — too frightened to even try to open his eyes.

Only his emergency parachute had come out at the last instant. Otherwise he would have flown clear over the highway, too.

"It felt like I had been smacked in the face by a two-by-four." He thought he was blind. He was sure his nose was broken.

"Open your eyes!" shouted a rescue worker.

Rose finally did. He saw two police cars. The policemen were arguing about which one would give him a ticket for entering a thorough-fare away from a legal intersection.

Neither one did, as things turned out. Both policemen understood that it had been an accident.

Rose recovered quickly, though he still has a scar across his eyes from the crash.

With the help of famous dragster drivers Marvin Schwartz and Don Garlits, the Monster was rebuilt. "We put that hummer back together for the next weekend," said Rose.

Rose continued to drive for Arfons for another two years. There were only four jet cars in the world and they were in constant demand at drag strips and oval courses. They weren't racing each other, but only making high-speed exhibition runs.

And burning cars.

A derelict car would be chained to the back of the jet car in the middle of the infield. All of the track lights would then be turned off. In the darkness, the crowd could hear the sound of the jet engine as it increased in speed. Then the driver would flip on the afterburner.

Burning cars is one of the most spectacular stunts of a jet dragster.

With a thundering howl, a great 30-foot-long arrow of fire would shoot out the back. The sound would frighten and stun the crowd. In seconds, the car would be melted to the ground in a shower of fire and sparks.

Car burnings are still an exciting part of jet car exhibitions. But they have always been somewhat embarrasing to Doug Rose. He prefers to make high-speed runs on the track. Still, Rose considers himself to be an entertainer. If the crowds and the promoters are will-

41

ing to pay large fees for this extra feature, he'll do it.

Tragedy struck Rose in 1966. It was at a track in Richlands, Virginia. Rose and his wife were there to put on a jet exhibition for a new track. The track had been built with the guard rails next to the pavement. Usually the guard rails are farther back from the track.

It was a gloomy, rainy, wet day. The crowd was there to see the Green Monster. Any thought Rose had of postponing his exhibition faded as the crowd grew more and more restive. He talked to his wife. Conditions were very dangerous. The track was wet. In the uphill shutoff area there was a great puddle. He would be slowing down in more than an inch of water.

The decision was his. He decided to go for it. He decided to make an easy run just to please the crowd. He would make a great deal of fire and sound. But he wouldn't be going very fast.

Later, he knew that if he had gone faster his parachute might have saved him. But he was doing less than 100 miles per hour when he passed the finish line. The Green Monster rose up on the water and began to come around. Rose knew he was losing control. Quickly he popped the parachute, but he was going too slow for it to have an immediate effect.

Though by then he was traveling at a relatively slow speed, the unprotected front of the Monster climbed up on the steel guard rail. The car slid along the rail for several yards before it dropped back to the track.

Then it started to roll slowly back down the hill. Rose reached for the brake pedal to stop it. He couldn't, but at first he didn't understand why. Turning the wheel, he guided the car to a soft stop against the rail. Then he looked down into the cockpit.

"The rail ripped the bottom front of the cockpit off, where my legs were," Rose said. "They went right away. I didn't know it, but they did hurt a lot. I was trying to stop the car. I was kind of numb. I could see the ground but I couldn't see the ends of my legs."

Both of Rose's legs were lost, below his knees.

43

Doug Rose is not a man to bemoan his fate. He quickly learned how to use artificial limbs. The accident was in July and by September he was back in his jet car. He even drove himself home from the hospital on the very day he received his new legs. Today he helps other new amputees accept what has happened to them.

Rose is a perfect example of overcoming a handicap. He refused to allow his accident to slow him down. Today he walks straight and tall, without a limp.

During the difficult days, his dream about a Green Mamba jet car became stronger and stronger. He could see the green scales and the huge engine. He knew every rivet and every weld. He had become an expert on jet engines. He could take a wrecked J-47 engine and totally rebuild it for jet car use.

In his garage in California, where he goes for the winter, he has several J-47 engines. Some are used, some are brand-new. All will be used for jet cars sooner or later.

Gradually the Green Mamba became a reality and Doug Rose went on his own. In July,

The Green Mamba thunders away in a winning drag race against another jet car.

1968, he made his first run in the Green Mamba at Fremont, California. Mamba has been thrilling crowds ever since, with Rose at the wheel.

Doug Rose loves the feel of the great accceleration. It presses him into the cockpit seat with several G forces. He can hear the air howling past his head into the jet intake. He can

When Rose flips the switch there is a roll of thunder and a flash of fire.

hear the thunder of the afterburner at the rear. When he flashes across the finish line he is in a world of his own.

It is a very fast world. Once at Sacramento, California, he drove over *297 miles per hour* in a *quarter mile.* He became the fastest jet dragster driver ever.

Rose plans to continue with jet cars. He once wanted to break the land speed record for jet cars, but then along came rockets. Eventually he hopes to manage a team of jet cars. He'll hire other drivers and he'll run the operation. That is, if he can stay out of the cockpit long enough to get used to a desk.

46

3

LT. COL. ELDON JOERSZ

The beautiful but deadly looking SR-71 Blackbird has been around for a number of years. But many things about it are still secret. Few people even knew it was in the Air Force until 1981. That year another country fired a heat-seeking missile at an SR-71 during a reconnaissance mission.

But the missile missed. In fact, it exploded several miles away from the Blackbird.

Oh, the missile arrived at the right spot in the sky. It was just that the Blackbird was long gone by then.

The SR-71 Blackbird is the fastest, highest-

Captain Eldon W. Joersz (right) and Major George T. Morgan and the sleek Blackbird that holds the air speed record for airplanes. At right rear are the shelters to keep the planes from prying eyes.

flying airplane in the world today. The pilots who fly it, and one pilot and one radar officer in particular, are among the best and most skilled in the Air Force.

These two, Lt. Col. Eldon W. Joersz and Major George T. Morgan, flew the Blackbird faster than any airplane has ever been flown before. Joersz (a captain at that time) was the pilot and Morgan the RSO (radar systems officer).

The record, set on July 28, 1976, still stands today as the absolute world speed record for airplanes.

At Lockheed Aircraft Company they have a division called "The Skunk Works." In this design and engineering section they work on the most exotic airplanes. This section is where the famous F-104 Starfighter was designed and built. So was the triple-sonic (three times the speed of sound) YF-12A Interceptor. Other famous airplanes like the U-2 spyplane were designed and built by Lockheed's Skunk Works.

And so was the speedy Blackbird.

In flight, the Blackbird looks deadly, but it is really a reconnaissance airplane.

The Blackbird is a strange mixture of future and past. Look at how it finds its way around. Most airplanes do this by radio beams and homing devices. The Blackbird has a system that remembers the exact location of 52 stars. Just take it up where it can "see" the sky with its equipment and it can find its way. It needs no help from the ground at all. A part of this system is a clock that is accurate to 5 milliseconds (the blink of an eye). Between the clock and the star finder, the Blackbird can go anywhere in the world and arrive at any *exact* spot. It doesn't even need the pilot or the RSO to find its way. They just tell it where to go, and it goes there.

Yet on the ground the Blackbird often sits in a huge pool of its own fuel. The airplane is built with the outer skin as the outside of the fuel tanks. Since it must endure temperatures from cold (on the ground) to very hot (in supersonic flight) the skin shrinks and expands. So the fuel tanks leak on the ground.

When they heat up in high-speed flight, they seal. Meanwhile, the airplane must use a fuel with a higher flash point. This means a fuel that doesn't burn very easily. Otherwise any carelessly tossed cigarette or spark could set it on fire on the ground.

"It's enough to give a safety officer a heart

attack the first time he sees this," said one SR-71 pilot with a laugh. But with the special fuel, fire accidents don't happen.

Flying the SR-71 is very complex. Pilots, including Joersz and Morgan, must go through a special routine before each flight.

In fact, each flight of this airplane really begins long before takeoff. In those hours before the mission there are a series of tests and checks that no other airplane in the world must go through. Ground crews need many hours to install the computer tapes that will control the mission. Special secret sensors are put into position on the Blackbird.

Then everything must be checked and double-checked. The oil that is added to the engines is almost *solid.* On a warm summer day it must still be heated before the engines will turn over.

Meanwhile, the pilot and the RSO begin their preparation for each flight three hours before takeoff. First they eat a high protein breakfast of steak and eggs. It is the same breakfast served astronauts. In fact, SR-71 pilots are as

52

Blairsville Junior High School
Blairsville, Pennsylvania

A nose view of the Blackbird showing the flat projections out to each side.

close to astronauts as one can be. They have their own special skills for flying higher than the stratosphere, but lower than deep space, where the air is very thin.

About an hour and a half before the flight, both crewmen are given extensive physical examinations. Then they begin to "suit up" in special full-pressure space suits. These suits will protect the crew and allow them to complete their mission even if the cockpit is damaged and pressure is lost.

53

Silhouetted in the setting sun, the Blackbird is refueled in the air for an endurance flight.

Two men are needed to assist the crew in donning their suits. The process takes about 30 minutes. It includes pressure tests, breathing checks, space suit air-conditioning checks, and faceplate heating tests (to prevent fogging).

The crew is then transported to their SR-71 in a van. They can plug their suits into the van's system for cooling.

Each Blackbird has its own shelter hangar at Beale Air Force Base in California. Although there are Blackbirds flying reconnaissance missions around the world, they are all based at

Beale. They may land elsewhere, but their home is Beale. On very long missions, they are refueled by flying tankers.

Strapping into the cockpit of an SR-71 Blackbird is a difficult job. The crew becomes almost a part of the plane. Ground crewmen assist and soon the air crew is sealed in and breathing pure oxygen. Flight controls are in the front seat. The RSO has no flight controls, but he can control the horizontal flight of the plane through his navigation instruments.

Captain Joersz and Major Morgan went through all of this before their record-breaking flight. They knew they would soon be flying more than 15 miles above the ground. They would be moving through the air at a speed more than three times the speed of sound. Their 130,000-pound airplane would be streaking through space faster than a 30.06 rifle bullet.

Every *second* they would be moving nearly 3,300 feet. That's almost the length of *three* dragstrips each second.

With the oil heated to a liquid, they prepared

to start the engines. Because of the high flash point of the fuel, triethyl borane (TEB) is injected into the engine. TEB catches fire upon contact with JP-7 fuel. This ignites the fuel.

The first engine is started, then the crew waits two minutes. This gets the hydraulic systems operating. Flight controls can then be checked. Then the second engine is started.

For 15 more minutes, more tests are made. Finally the plane is taxied to the runway.

Joersz ran the engines up to military power. This is maximum power without the afterburners. He held the brakes while more systems were checked. Then he shoved the throttles forward into the afterburner range.

The howling engines boomed as each after-

A parachute mounted in the center rear is used to slow the Blackbird during her landing rollout. It is dropped off before the airplane stops.

burner lit off. Joersz let off the brakes. They wouldn't hold the huge airplane with the burners on, anyhow.

Quickly the Blackbird picked up speed. The two J-58 jet engines were putting out 68,000 pounds of thrust. The airplane moved faster and faster. In 20 seconds Blackbird was airborne.

On the ground in the western United States a 15 and 25 kilometer straight-line course had been laid out. Speed record attempts between airplanes and nations have never been unusual. Each nation wants the record for her own planes. The United States was preparing for a final, all-out assault on the absolute speed record.

Meanwhile, in 1974, one Blackbird had sped from New York to London. This established a new world speed record. The flight was made in only one hour and 56 minutes. The pilot was Major James V. Sullivan and the RSO was Major Noel F. Widdifield.

This flight cut nearly *three hours* off the previous record. It was held by a British F-4K fighter and had been set in 1969.

Then the same SR-71 was flown from London to Los Angeles. The airplane arrived in Los Angeles almost four hours before it took off from London. It had beaten the sun and the clock. The whole flight, with one slow-down period for air refueling, took only three hours, 47 minutes. Another speed record had been set. The pilot was Captain Harold B. Adams and the RSO Major William C. Machorek.

These flights were for training purposes — and to break records. The Soviet Union was also flying high and fast. During this time a stripped-down E266 Foxbat, a Russian fighter, was making record-breaking flights.

The SR-71 would break a record, then the

Russians would come back with a MIG-25 or a Foxbat and break the SR-71's record. Thundering back, the SR-71 Blackbird would break that record.

The flights scheduled over the measured kilometers were to capture the records once and for all.

Captain Joersz and Major Morgan did just that. Once and for all. The Russians haven't tried since those "faster than a speeding bullet" flights in 1976. Joersz flew the Blackbird at an amazing 2,194 miles per hour. This was a new air speed record.

This is not to say that the Blackbird won't fly faster. The military is cagey about the ultimate speed. Why go faster, they want to know? They already have the world air speed record. If the Russians go faster, they hint, then they'll roll out the Blackbird to fly for the record again over the measured course. They speak with confidence, as though regaining the record wouldn't be too difficult.

Joersz received the De La Vaulx Medal for his record-breaking flight. So did two other SR-71

A black needle in flight, the SR-71 Blackbird holds many flight endurance and altitude records as well as the air speed record.

pilots on that same day. One was for horizontal altitude flight (Capt. Robert C. Helt, pilot, and RSO Maj. Larry A. Elliott). Another was for speed over a closed course (Maj. Adolphus H. Bledsoe, Jr., pilot, and RSO Maj. John T. Fuller). The De La Vaulx Medal, named for Comte De La Vaulx who was an air pioneer, is awarded in France for aircraft world records.

Captain Joersz was promoted to major and then, later, to lieutenant colonel. He became the commander of the only squadron of SR-71s in the world, at Beale AFB. He still flies the speedy airplane, but now he is in command of all the other Blackbird pilots and RSOs as well.

He recently received a letter from a 16-year-old high school student. The student wanted to become an SR-71 pilot, the cream of the Air Force pilots. Colonel Joersz remembered his own days as a youngster dreaming of flying the fastest airplanes.

He advised the young student to study math and engineering, and stressed the importance of keeping grades high. Then he suggested that he enroll in the Air Force Academy. Again, he said to work hard and keep his grades as high as possible.

After the Air Force Academy, he said to become an Air Force pilot. Try to become the best possible pilot, and work toward piloting high-performance fighter planes. The next step would be to try to get into the Advance Flight School at Edwards Air Force Base in California. This is the school of the Air Force's test pilots. If you become one of the best of these pilots, he told the student, you could qualify to become a Blackbird pilot.

The student thanked Joersz for the advice.

He said he felt he could do it. He would try.

But wait a minute. What does an SR-71 Blackbird *do?* What is its *job* in the United States Air Force? Why all this speed, and secrecy about equipment? The Blackbird is not an airplane they like to talk about freely.

The SR-71 is obviously a spyplane. The Air Force won't say, exactly. It has no guns. It is designed to fly in before or after a battle, not during. It is designed to take pictures and do other measuring tasks with its secret equipment. They do say that one of the cameras on the SR-71 can take a picture from 15 miles up and while the airplane is going more than 2,000 miles per hour. In the photo you can identify people at a backyard barbecue. Since the airplane is used for reconnaissance, such a camera is necessary.

There is more, much more. But details are not discussed. Other equipment, other systems, will give even more information about what's on the ground. And perhaps even hide the Blackbird while it is doing its job.

4

CRAIG BREEDLOVE

On one land speed record run, the car was destroyed. It was actually sunk in a salt water pool several feet deep.

But the driver, Craig Breedlove, was not injured.

What seemed even more important to Breedlove, he set a new land speed record on that very same run.

Land speed record attempts are never without danger or drama. This one, though, was more exciting than usual.

Craig Breedlove was a picture of the typical

Craig Breedlove

64

land speed record holder. He was handsome and popular. He knew how to act the part of a speed hero. He was a daredevil in every sense. Yet he was always a very careful craftsman when building his beautiful cars. With them he held several records, including the one above. More about that later.

When he was a young man, Breedlove knew he wanted to set a land speed record on the Bonneville salt. In fact, he had memorized all the records set by the daredevils before him.

He knew that the last American to hold the land speed record was Ray Keech. That had been in 1928. Keech had thundered his famed White Triplex to an astounding speed of just over 203 miles per hour.

But then along came the English. The land speed record became their property alone.

In 1929, Major H.O.D. Segrave drove more than 231 miles per hour. Then came Sir Malcolm Campbell in the years from 1931 to 1937. Campbell upped the speed record to 301.42 miles per hour. In 1937 (the year Craig Breedlove was born) Captain G.E.T. Eyston captured the coveted record with a speed of 311.42 miles per hour.

In 1938 and 1939 there was a seesaw battle between Eyston and another Englishman, John Cobb. Cobb finally settled the matter with a blazing speed of 368.9 miles per hour.

Cobb's record stood until 1947 when he broke his own record with a speed of 394.2 miles per hour. On one of the two runs he had gone over 400 miles per hour.

There the record stood. No man had gone faster. No machine had been built that could challenge the speed. A ten-year-old Craig Breedlove knew of all these records. As he grew through high school, he watched to see if anybody could break them. All the time he knew that he, himself, would eventually try.

When he was 16 years old, Breedlove built his first speed car. He won a trophy by driving his hot rod 103 miles per hour. He graduated from high school and went to work as a welder for a builder of custom cars. Then he took a job in the engineering department of an aircraft manufacturer. This was a major industry in

Southern California where he lived.

Meanwhile, speedster Mickey Thompson streaked across the Bonneville salt in his four-engine Challenger. His speed was over 400 miles per hour. But Thompson was unable to get turned around and on a return run in the required time. Cobb's record still stood.

Craig Breedlove decided to design and build his own land speed record car. The reaction of his friends was laughter.

Everybody knew that land speed records were not won by hot-rodders throwing together a car. LSR cars were very complex. They cost hundreds of thousands of dollars.

Who was Craig Breedlove to think he could go against men like Campbell, Eyston, and Cobb? Who was he to think he could outrace the great Mickey Thompson?

Breedlove continued to design his car. He switched from piston engine to jet for one reason. He had very little money. Jet engines cost less for the amount of power they deliver. He built a model. Then he talked his friends at the aircraft company into running wind tunnel

Craig Breedlove decided to build his own speed record car, and he *did*.

tests on it. He named the car Spirit of America. The model showed a fast-looking, three-wheeled car.

Over 100 tests later, Breedlove was satisfied. But by then his money was gone. Yet by then he was totally committed to the Spirit of America project.

So Craig Breedlove sold almost everything he owned. This included his home and furniture. He *had* to keep going.

He took his model and his plans and walked the streets, searching for a sponsor. Door after door was closed to him. Finally he wandered into the Shell Oil Company District Office in Santa Monica, California. He announced himself to a receptionist, asking simply for the man in charge.

Fate plays strange tricks. The man in charge had the same name. He thought his secretary was announcing a relative. He asked Breedlove in. When he realized the young driver was there to sell him something, he limited him to only ten minutes.

This was a stroke of courtesy that has since brought millions of dollars of publicity and good will to the company.

Breedlove began to talk about his idea. Ten minutes stretched into a half hour, then an hour. Shell Oil gave the go-ahead and that prompted Goodyear Tire and Rubber to enter the project. The great, long, smooth car was completed.

In August, 1962, the team reported to the Bonneville Salt Flats. The course was dragged to smooth the rough salt. Timing lights were set up. Everything seemed ready.

But it was no use. The car wasn't ready. It veered off the course at only 300 miles per hour. The brake system wasn't working properly. Sadly, the crew packed up and headed for home. They knew it would be another year before they could be ready.

In July, 1963, they returned. The car had been changed. The brakes had been improved. The front wheel had been made steerable. The throttle had been moved from hand to foot. A huge tail fin had been added. The car had been turned into a giant arrow.

Breedlove thundered over the measured mile at a speed of 388.47 miles per hour. The return run was equally perfect but much faster at 428.37. In fact, that is why two runs must be made for an official record. Course conditions must be taken into account, including important factors like tail wind speeds.

The average for Breedlove's two runs was 407.45 miles per hour. Craig Breedlove had become the first man to go more than 400 miles per hour on a two-run average.

From a high school boy's dreaming about it,

he had become the holder of the world land speed record. Spirit of America and her driver went on tour.

Meanwhile, other drivers weren't sitting at home doing nothing. Walt and Art Arfons of Akron, Ohio, were building their own land speed vehicles. *Two* of them, one for each.

So Breedlove headed for home to work on Spirit. He improved the car with a new J-47 jet engine and new streamlining. He knew that either of the Arfons brothers could break his record and he wanted to be ready.

In September, 1964, Walt Arfons drove his jet-powered Wingfoot Express to a new land speed record of 413.2 miles per hour. Then Art Arfons drove the Green Monster to another new land speed record of 434.02 miles per hour. The speed record duel was becoming very exciting and very dangerous.

Craig Breedlove was ready with his new Spirit of America. On October 13, 1964, he waited as his crew bolted the canopy into place. He was no longer the holder of the land speed record. He knew what he had to do.

The first Spirit of America thunders through the measured mile, just at the first marker. A new land speed record was set, followed by a dive into a salt pool.

Releasing his brakes, he aimed Spirit for her first run over the measured mile 4½ miles away. Through the traps thundered the great white car. He popped his parachute and slowed to a stop. Then he waited for the speed for the first run. It finally came as the crew worked to get ready for the second run.

It was 442.59 miles per hour. He was halfway to a new record.

The second run started and a few seconds later the Spirit of America streaked through the measured mile. Nobody could believe their eyes. It took Breedlove less than *8 seconds* to get through the traps one mile apart. The speed was an amazing 498.13 miles per hour.

Was Breedlove satisfied? No. He knew that his mighty car could go even faster. Two days later he roared over the measured mile twice again. The speed for the first run was flashed down to the turnaround area. He'd gone 513.33 miles per hour. He was within one more run of breaking the "impossible" 500 miles per hour barrier.

The return run started. As he completed his run through the timing lights, the speed was flashed to the crew. It was 539.89 miles per hour. Breedlove had done it! The crew jumped and leaped and slapped each other on the back.

Wait till Craig got back to the pits! They'd *mob* him.

But there was *trouble* out on the course!

The great white car was not slowing down! When it should have been coasting to a stop, it was still going over 300 miles per hour!

The braking parachute had torn away. Then the emergency chute had torn free. At over 500 miles per hour, Breedlove had instantly burned away his brakes. He was hurtling along with no way to stop and the end of the salt flats approaching.

The crew watched in horror as Spirit rushed along. Inside the cockpit, Breedlove veered the car to one side, hoping to slow it. It snapped through a telephone pole like a toothpick. He veered it back and forth again. Finally the car plowed through over a quarter mile of standing water. Then it tore through an 8 foot-high bank of salt. Finally it sailed over *100 yards* through the air and nosed into an 18 foot-deep pond of salt water.

Instantly everything was silent. Only an echo of the Spirit's thundering engine bounced off the mountains miles away.

In the cockpit, Breedlove had felt himself flying through the air. Below was water. He had reached up and flipped open the cockpit canopy. As the water rushed in, he swam out. Soon only the tail section of the car remained above the water's surface. But Craig Breedlove, with a new land speed record, was safe on the salt shore.

"I'm alright . . . what's the speed?" he shouted as his worried crew rushed to the scene.

Breedlove, left, and two of his crew stare sadly at the mostly submerged Spirit of America.

Breedlove thundered back in Spirit of America Sonic I to recapture the world land speed record for jet cars. He is shown doing it here.

Art Arfons was impressed, but not frightened. He raised the record to 536 mph. Craig Breedlove built a new four-wheeled vehicle, named it Spirit of America Sonic I, and took back the record. His speed was 555. Only 72 hours later Arfons went 576.

Craig Breedlove came back again. Though his car was by then rising up off the salt like an airplane, he drove an astounding 600.601 miles per hour. As he had broken the 400 and 500

76

miles per hour barriers, he also broke the 600 miles per hour barrier.

This new land speed record for jet cars has remained in the name of Craig Breedlove. Art Arfons destroyed his car and seriously injured himself in a spectacular, mile-long, end-over-end accident. One wheel from the car flew up and went through the blades — *between* them — of an overhead helicopter. Another wheel flew *four miles* from the scene.

Arfons had once asked Breedlove, "Are both of us just going to continue this until one of us either crashes or kills himself?"

"I don't know, Art, I guess so," Breedlove had answered.

And so it has been.

But the story isn't over. Craig Breedlove is now building a new car. He calls the car Spirit of America Sonic II. The car will be rocket powered. Breedlove wants to officially break the speed of sound on land. His model is finished and his money is arranged.

If his past is any indication of his future, Breedlove will continue until he reaches this lightning-fast new goal.

Lee Taylor

5

LEE TAYLOR

The sleek jet-powered boat Hustler roared faster and faster. In the cockpit, Lee Taylor studied the water. He glanced at his instruments. Everything looked OK.

The Lake Havasu, Arizona, shores flashed past so fast that he felt he was in a long tunnel. But then things began to go wrong. A mountain appeared dead ahead. The boat was out of control. Taylor remembered the moment long after the 1964 run.

"I wanted no part of climbing that mountain in my boat," he said. So he bailed out at more than 200 miles per hour. The boat roared on to shatter itself on the rocks. Taylor skipped across the water's surface like a flat stone. He bounced on the concrete-hard water again and again. Then he, too, hit the rocks.

Eighteen hours later he awoke in a hospital. He was a near-vegetable. He had bones broken throughout his body. He couldn't talk. He couldn't even remember the names of his children. The dream of Lee to become the fastest man in the world on water seemed over.

Hustler was gone and he was terribly hurt.

But nobody took into consideration the determination of Lee Taylor. All his life he had loved competition. In school in Southern California he had been an athletic star. He was on the football team and other teams. He went on to become a star player on the tough University of Washington Huskies football team. Then he became a professional football player for awhile.

Taylor loved the idea of hitting harder, of lasting longer, of going faster—*especially* of going faster. He had always wanted to go faster than anybody else.

So he took up drag boat racing at nearby

Long Beach Marine Stadium. By then Taylor had a family, but he couldn't stay away from dangerous sports. He became a drag boat winner.

Then he took up water skiing. Again he wanted to be the fastest of all. Finally, on the ragged edge of control, he raced to a speed of 92 miles per hour on water skis. It was a new world water ski speed record.

Taylor *loved* the feeling of being fastest.

But all this time, Lee Taylor had a dream he held deep inside. He wanted to be the fastest man on water. He wanted to build a boat and go faster than anybody had ever gone before.

So he began to build Hustler. The boat was practically all jet engine. It was a big jet engine that floated. And it had a cockpit for Taylor. It was a missile on water.

But during a test run in 1964, Taylor had his terrible accident. The boat had run perfectly but it hadn't slowed down as quickly as it should. Taylor had worried more about going fast than about slowing down. He had been forced to jump from the boat. When they finally got to him, he was almost dead.

To make matters even worse, the helicopter rushing him to the hospital crashed. It was a very bad day for Taylor all around. Everybody said that if he lived, he would never be the same. They said he would never walk, for one thing. Nor be able to work to support himself. He would probably be in bed, or in a wheelchair, for the rest of his life.

They didn't know Lee Taylor. Even then the dream was still burning inside him.

He wanted to be the fastest man on water. He'd come close, very close. And he'd paid dearly for the effort so far. He wanted to keep trying.

It took him *three years* to get better. He worked and exercised. He forced his broken body to do what he wanted it to do. He suffered constant pain and often he felt he was losing the battle, but he kept trying.

Meanwhile he was having Hustler rebuilt. Eventually he began working on the boat himself. As his own body recovered, he rebuilt Hustler.

In June, 1967, Lee Taylor rocketed Hustler across the glassy surface of Lake Gunterville in

Alabama. On shore his crew watched tensely. Taylor was carrying the scars from his crash. His left eye permanently looked to the left. But otherwise he was in good health. So was Hustler.

On that hot and humid day Lee Taylor set a new world water speed record of 285.213 miles per hour. He had accomplished his great dream. Everything, he felt, had been worth it. The pain and suffering were behind him. He was the fastest man on water.

Lee Taylor was happy, but not completely satisfied. He knew that sooner or later somebody would come along and break his record. That is the way the world of speed works. He knew that speed records never last forever. The people who try to break speed records are driven by things deep inside them. They will put everything they own into an attempt to break a record. Nothing seems to stop them. Breaking a record is the single most important thing in their lives.

So Taylor knew that eventually somebody would go for his record.

He had a new boat in mind. It would be a

Taylor's dream boat ready for blast-off. This was the first rocket-powered boat in the world.

"super boat." His new boat would be a needle-shaped missile that would skim across the water at a tremendous speed. In his heart he could see his new dream boat breaking the speed of sound. He could see it going *twice* as fast as his current record. Even *faster.*

How does it feel to travel so fast over water? Lee Taylor explained the feeling to writer Al Carr of the *Los Angeles Times.*

"There is no sound. Everything is behind you. It's just you. You have a feeling of wanting to go faster. You have a strong desire to go faster.

84

You are euphoric. You want the feeling to continue."

Taylor's record stood for eleven years. Others tried, but nobody could go faster on water than Lee Taylor's 285 miles per hour.

Then it happened. In 1978 an Australian driver named Ken Warby broke Taylor's record. In fact, he shattered it. He raced his jet-powered boat to an incredible 317.60 miles per hour. He was the new world water speed record king. Taylor was only the *second* fastest man on water.

This was not something that Lee Taylor could live with. He knew he had to bring his dream boat to reality. He said, "I will bring the water speed record back to the United States."

Taylor knew that jet power was fast, but that rocket power would be even faster. And a rocket engine is smaller and lighter. You wouldn't have to float a rocket engine like you had to do with a jet engine. You could build a superfast boat and put a rocket engine into it.

The engine Taylor picked for his U.S. Discovery II was an 8,000-pound thrust, 16,000-

Left: The business end of U.S. Discovery II houses the Woodruff Rocket engine. The four-inch skeg is below the engine. Right: In the nose is the 50-gallon fuel tank.

horsepower Woodruff Rocket. It had been designed for aircraft and missile use. It was very powerful, but only a couple of feet long.

Taylor worked on his new boat, no matter what happened. He ran low on money. He borrowed more. He went from company to company to get sponsorship help. He *had* to bring the record back to the United States.

Gradually sponsors appeared and the boat

took shape. It was a beautiful boat. It was 40 feet long and had a missile nose. It looked like something out of the future. It was made of aluminum and had two stabilizing sponsons to each side of the cockpit. A 9 foot-high fin at the rear would help to keep the boat in a straight line at high speed.

Two 50-gallon fuel tanks were designed to feed hydrogen peroxide (H_2O_2) under high pressure to the rocket. A jet engine takes air into the front through an intake. A rocket engine does not. It is closed at the front and burns only the fuel that enters. In both cases, gases are shot out the rear at extremely high speeds. This forces the engine (and the vehicle) forward.

Taylor planned to stop his boat with drogue parachutes just like most other speed vehicles. At first the boat would sink back into the water and slow down. Then the parachute would help to stop it by popping out at the right time.

At high speed, the entire boat would be up out of the water except for the little stainless steel "skeg" at the rear. It extended four inches below the lowest point on the hull. At full

This is the custom trailer built for hauling the U.S. Discovery II. It is shown top on and top off, with the boat inside.

speed, the skeg was to act as a "fixed guidance system." It wouldn't move, nor could Taylor guide it from the cockpit. It would be the only part of the entire 5,000-pound boat in the water. Otherwise, the boat would be a missile skimming along just over the water.

88

To qualify for the water speed record, at least one part of the boat had to be in the water, of course.

Taylor tested his boat again and again on the smooth waters of Walker Lake in California. It was fast — faster than even he had imagined. Without effort it would skim across the water at tremendous speeds. One run was timed at over 333 miles per hour. Taylor insisted that the throttle wasn't nearly open for that run.

On another run Taylor would only call the speed "fantastic." Much later that speed leaked out. It was reported to have been *over 400 miles per hour.*

An enthusiastic Taylor and his crew moved to Lake Tahoe for the official record runs. Sponsors wanted the runs there, even though the water wasn't quite as smooth. The course was marked out and timing equipment set up.

With reporters and photographers and television cameras waiting, the decision to go was finally made. The record seemed within grasp. Everything was working well. Everybody believed that the record would return to the United

States on that bright November day in 1980 —
even if the water wasn't *perfectly* smooth.

Before the record run, Taylor was asked what
was next. What did he plan to do after that day,
after he had broken the water speed record?

"Break the *sound* barrier, going 1,000 miles
per hour in U.S. Discovery III," he replied
happily.

At first everything went well. The team
planned to work their way up to the speed
record through a series of timed runs. Though

Taylor's final high-speed run with the sponsons completely out of the water and only the skeg carrying the boat. A shock wave kicks up water under the nose.

there was an unpleasant set of tiny waves on the lake, the boat came up to speed smoothly. It skimmed through the measured course for a timed run. Then it turned to come back, and again a run was timed. The average speed of this first set was more than 265 miles per hour.

But as the boat began to slow down from the second run, it started to wobble. It was still traveling terribly fast. It seemed to bounce from one sponson to the other.

Then suddenly one sponson dug into the

water. That hurtled the boat the other way. It tipped up and flashed end over end at very high speed. From shore, onlookers watched in horror as the boat exploded.

A wire service helicopter clattered in to see if they could help. One reporter aboard saw debris and nothing else. Then Lee Taylor's helmet popped to the surface to float among parts of U.S. Discovery II. There was no sign of Taylor.

Lee Taylor's body, still strapped in the cockpit, was found several days later on the bottom of Lake Tahoe. His quest for the water speed record had ended.

Officially the record will have to be broken by somebody else. But unofficially, observers are certain that Lee Taylor had gone well over the record several times before he crashed. Many consider him to be fastest on water even if he doesn't hold the official record. And even though he gave his life in doing it.

6

GARY GABELICH

"five ... four ... three ... two ... one ... *ignition!*"

Gary Gabelich punched a button on the dashboard. He felt The Blue Flame leap forward as fuel rushed into the rocket engine. He was pressed back into his seat so hard he couldn't move.

He felt the excitement rush through him as it did each time a run started. Faster and faster the needle-shaped car raced.

Before he could even think about it, he was rocketing at more than 300 miles per hour over the salt of the Bonneville Salt Flats. By then it

Gary Gabelich

94

was totally quiet inside the cockpit. He could hear nothing. He was running ahead of the thundering sound of his engine. He was on the second, final run. This was it!

Ahead, he could see the big plywood billboards marking the entrance to the timing traps. His airspeed indicator read 610 miles per hour. He had two seconds of fuel left.

He was *far* from the day in grade school when as a boy he had made a drawing instead of doing his math problems. But there was a connection. For on that day years before Gary Gabelich had drawn a picture of a sleek rocket car.

"I was drawing cars," Gabelich recalled, "when I should have been paying attention to arithmetic." But he said to himself, "I want to be the fastest man in the world."

Handsome Gary Gabelich grew up in San Pedro, California. He was raised with his sister, Judy. His mother was Mexican-American and his father was Yugoslavian. That's where the name Gabelich came from.

"But people have trouble with Gabelich," he

said "I've heard everything from Grabbel-scratch to Gobbylitch." That was at the beginning. Few people in the world of land speed records have trouble with the name now. It is etched firmly into the books.

Some people also choose to use Gabelich's *other* name. In the past few years he has also become known as "Rocketman."

From that day in school, Gabelich's interest in cars increased. His father took him to a racetrack in Los Angeles. He looked through the fence and saw the cars roaring around the track. "Boy! That looks *dangerous!*" he said, "But I bet it would be a lot of fun."

He drove in his first drag race when he was a high school student in Long Beach, California. He was only 16 years old. But he won a trophy. If he wasn't sure before, that did it. He knew he wanted to be a race driver. That was how he wanted to spend his life.

Gabelich became a "gofer" for racing teams when he was 17. This is the one on the team who runs for parts and carries coffee and donuts to the mechanics. Gabelich liked what he was doing. But he really wanted to drive. Deep down inside, he still wanted to be the fastest man on earth.

When he was 18 years old, Gary Gabelich got a chance to drive a jet car. He won the first ever drag race between two jet cars. He traveled 246 miles per hour to do it. He covered the quarter-mile dragstrip in only 6.47 seconds.

"From then on," he remembers, "I *really* had the bug."

But auto racing has never been a high-paying job for beginners. So when he graduated from high school in 1959, Gabelich went to work for North American Aviation. He started as a mail boy.

Gabelich is smart and a hard worker. He feels good when he is working hard. Promotions came quickly. He moved up to planner. Then he was assigned to the Apollo moon project as a coordinator. Next he became a staff assistant to one of the project managers.

Then he became a test astronaut. He was back in the type of work he loved best. It was dangerous, challenging, high-speed work. He spent time in pressure chambers. He was dropped from airplanes. It was exciting work that could eventually have led to a trip to the moon.

But Gabelich had not been standing still in his off-duty hobbies. North American was not taking every minute of his day. Off duty he took part in auto racing.

In 1960, he drove in the first side-by-side, twin-engined supercharged dragster race in the world. He won this and many other races on drag strips.

He was the driver of a successful A-Fuel dragster in 1961.

In 1962 he held both the top speed and low-elapsed time records at San Fernando Raceway in Southern California.

In 1963 he won the first United Drag Racing Association sanctioned meet. He continued as a winner on drag strips.

In 1967 he became the first dragster driver to break drag racing's 7-second barrier.

Through these years, Gabelich was dreaming of the land speed record. He had always wanted to be the world's fastest man. The

Gabelich shortly after he set a new drag boat record of over 200 miles per hour in a quarter mile.

dream never seemed to die. Gabelich continued to set record after record on drag strips. He had turned to drag boats as well. He was the American Power Boat Association Blown Fuel and Gas National Drag Boat Champion in 1968. Then he became the first man to go over 200 miles per hour in a quarter-mile drag boat competition in 1969.

On land and on water, nothing could slow down Gary Gabelich.

At last his chance came. He was well known in racing circles. Everybody knew that if a car had a chance to break a record, Gabelich was the driver to hire.

One of his backers wanted to build a rocket-powered boat.

"I went back to Milwaukee, Wisconsin, to a company called Reaction Dynamics, in 1968," said Gabelich. "They were working on The Blue Flame. I showed them a blueprint of the boat and said that we wanted a rocket to fit into it that would allow us to go 200-230 miles per hour."

Chuck Suba, who had been working on The Blue Flame and who was to be its driver, had been killed driving a dragster. Did Gary Gabelich want the job of driving The Blue Flame?

Of *course* he said. "I really wanted to drive that baby. I think I would have paid them for the opportunity. I had good vibes about the car even before it was completed.

"And . . . it looked like my drawing that I had done back in grade school."

Gabelich worked with the team to complete

the car. Then he drove it through a series of test runs at Bonneville.

"The car was so well designed that I didn't have to drive it. I just aimed it and made compensations for the driftage."

So came the day of the record attempt. The Blue Flame streaked past the big billboards in a blur. In the cockpit, Gabelich adjusted the wheel slightly. The world was rushing past him. The seconds ticked off in his brain almost too fast to count. He was out of the measured mile and watching the slow-down mileposts flash by. The first flew past at over 600 miles per hour.

His first run an hour ago had been a success. He had averaged 617.602 one way. But the rules required a round trip. The car had to be turned around and within one hour start off on its return run.

Another milepost flashed by and Gabelich reached up to punch a button. An explosive charge fired and a parachute popped out of the tail of The Blue Flame. Gabelich was jerked forward in his belts as the chute filled and the car slowed to 250 miles per hour.

With the first run a success, he needed this second one to set an official world speed record. Unofficial rocket speed runs had been made. Budweiser beer had sponsored a run with a rocket car and announced a new land speed record. But the run had been timed by Air Force radar over a very short distance. The rules require a one-mile distance to be timed, and by official clocks, not radar. The beer company car had made only a one-way run. The rules require a two-way run so that wind and other conditions can be averaged.

The Blue Flame streaks along at over 600 miles per hour

Many insisted that the beer company record was not official and should not be counted.

Another milepost flashed by and Gabelich fired out a second parachute. Again he was jerked forward in his seat belts. The car slowed to a mere 100 miles per hour. It looked almost as though he could get out and walk alongside. But Gabelich grinned to himself. He remembered the time he had been forced to bail out of a burning dragster going over 50 miles per hour. It had been no fun at all.

Gently Gabelich tapped his brakes and the

with Gabelich at the wheel.

Craig Breedlove (left), Ray Lavely, Sr. (center), and Gary Gabelich in the earlier days with Breedlove's short wheelbase dragster and Gabelich's glass-bodied Funny Car. Gabelich jumped from this car at over 50 miles per hour and it burned up.

car slowed even more. Finally it eased to a stop.

Soon the crew was swarming over the car. They were happy, for they had received the time from the officials. Gary Gabelich had managed 627.287 miles per hour on the return run. the two speeds averaged to a new world land speed record of 622.407 miles per hour. It was October 23, 1970.

Gabelich had become the fastest man in the world, officially. He was happy. He had accomplished his goal. He waved for his crew and the observers to be quiet. "I want to dedicate this run," he said, "to Chuck Suba and his mother and dad." Suba had been the planned driver of The Blue Flame. His parents had become friends with Gabelich and were there that day. Gary's own father grabbed Gary and hugged him.

Gabelich began touring with his car. He made speeches. Everywhere he went, people recognized Rocketman. He became famous. But he didn't stop racing.

In 1972 he was testing a new four-wheel-drive dragster in California. The car crashed. It was a terrible crash that destroyed the car. Gary Gabelich was removed from the burning wreckage. His left leg and foot were crushed. Worse, his left hand was cut off.

Doctors worked for hours over Gabelich. They saved his life. Then they repaired his crushed leg and foot. They sewed his hand back on. The operations worked. Today, Gabe-

The remains of Gabelich's four-wheel-drive dragster after the crash that cost him a severed hand and a crushed leg and foot.

lich is a racquetball champion using his sewed-on hand and his repaired leg. A trace of a scar all the way around his wrist is all that remains (though his legs are still scarred).

It wasn't long before Gabelich was racing in off-road races. These are some of the most punishing races of all on both car and driver. Again, he became a winner.

In spite of yet another serious accident in 1975, while driving a boat, Gabelich has continued to drive. In that accident his boat was shattered to pieces. Gabelich suffered internal injuries, a separated shoulder, and other cuts and bruises. Again he recovered in fine shape.

Other attempts are planned on the long-standing land speed record of Gary Gabelich. The Russians are planning an attempt. A British team has built a car and will try. Gabelich's friend, Craig Breedlove, is building a car to break the record.

To Gabelich, there is no choice. He, too, has a new car in the planning stages. He wants to break his own record. His car will be called The American Way.

"The Blue Flame was a fine piece of machinery, like a Swiss watch. The American Way will be even better because it will require specifications exceeding those that NASA had for their Apollo program.

"We chose the name The American Way because that's what our project is all about. It's overcoming adversity and working hard to

It wasn't long before Gabelich, in the cockpit, was back racing, this time off-road. At center is driver Mickey Thompson and at right is driver Parnelli Jones.

achieve a goal, a dream to do something that no one else has ever done and that *is* the American way," said Gary Gabelich.

He paused, then continued. "Some engineers believe that when I pass through the sound barrier the resulting shock wave will blow the car off the ground. Maybe, but I don't think so.

"In fact, I'm betting my life on it."

108

INDEX

Adams, Captain Harold B., 58
Advance Flight School, 61
American Power Boat Association, 99
American Way, The, 107
Arfons, Art, 28, 71, 76-77
Arfons, Walt, 35-40, 71

Beale Air Force Based, 54-55, 60
Blackbird, 47-62, 48, 50, 53, 54, 56-57, 60
Bledsoe, Maj. Adolphus H., Jr. 60
Blown Fuel and Gas National Drag Boat Champion, 99
Blue Flame, The, 93-108, 102-103
Bluebird, 18
Bonneville Salt Flats, 14, 17, 22-31, 65-67, 69-77, 93, 101-104
Breedlove, Craig, 8, 15, 28, 63-77, 64, 74, 104, 107

Campbell, Sir Donald, 18
Campbell, Sir Malcolm, 65, 67
Car burning, 40-42, 41
Carr, Al, 84
Challenger, 18, 67

Chrysler, 21-22
Cobb, John, 17, 66-67
Cook, Jim, 27-28

Daytona Beach, 17
De La Vaulx Medal, 59, 60
Discovery II, 11, 84-92, 86, 88, 90-91

E266 Foxbat, 58
Edwards Air Force Base, 61
El Mirage Dry Lake, 22
Elliott, Maj. Larry A., 60
Eyston, Captain G.E.T., 65-67

F4K fighter, 58
F7U Cutlass, 32
F-104 Starfighter, 49
Firestone Tire and Rubber Company, 22, 27
Fuller, Maj. John T., 60

Gabelich, Gary, 15, 93-108, 94, 104, 108
Garlits, Don, 40
"Gofer," 96
Goldenrod, 10, 16-31, 20, 23, 29, 30
Goodyear Tire and Rubber Company, 69

Green Mamba, 12, 32-46, 34, 39, 45, 46
Green Monster, 35-43, 71

Helt, Captain Robert C., 60
Hurst, George, 22
Hurst Performance Products, 22
Huskies (football team), 80
Hustler, 79-83

J-47 engine, 32, 44
J-58 engine, 56
JP-7 fuel, 56
Joersz, Lt. Col. Edwin, 15, 47-62, 48
Jones, Parnelli, 108

Keech, Ray, 65

Lake Gunterville, Alabama, 82-83
Lake Havasu, Arizona, 79
Lake Tahoe, 89
Lavely, Ray, Sr., 104
Lockheed Aircraft Company, 49
Long Beach, California, 96
Los Angeles Times, 84

Machorek, Major William C., 58
MIG-25, 59
Milwaukee, Wisconsin, 35, 100
Mobil Oil, 22
Morgan, Major George T., 48-60
Muroc Dry Lake, 22

National Jet Car Champion, 35
North American Aviation, 97

Pollywog, 24

Reaction Dynamics, 100
Richlands, Virginia, 42
Riverside International Raceway, 23
Rocketman, 96
Rose, Doug, 12, 15, 32-46, 33

San Fernando Raceway, 98
San Pedro, California, 95
Schwartz, Marvin, 40
Segrave, Major H.O.D., 65
Shell Oil Company, 69
"Skunk Works, The," 49
Spirit of America, 8, 63-77, 68, 72, 74, 76
SR-71. See Blackbird
Suba, Chuck, 100, 105
Sullivan, Major James V., 58
Summers, Bill and Bob, 10, 15, 19, 16-31, 20, 23

Tampa, Florida, 38
Taylor, Lee, 11, 15, 78-92
TEB. See Triethyl borane
Thompson, Mickey, 18, 67, 108
Traps, 14, 17, 73
Triethyl borane (TEB), 56

U-2 spyplane, 49
United Drag Racing Association, 98
University of Washington, 80

Walker Lake, 89
Warby, Ken, 85
Wendover Air Force Base, 26
White Triplex, 65
Widdifield, Major Noel F., 58
Wingfoot Express, 71
Woodruff Rocket, 86

110

Ross R. Olney is the author of more than ninety books for adults and young readers. He is an authority on sports and an expert on automobile and motorcycle racing. He has covered the major races for many years, and knows most of the drivers personally.

Previous titles include *Modern Auto Racing Superstars, Modern Motorcycle Superstars, Modern Drag Racing Superstars.*

Mr. Olney lives in Ventura, California, with his wife and two of their three sons.